BACK TO THE SOIL

A Journey of Resilience and Hope

Culture of Blessings INC

Founder: Bibi Alli

NEW YORK / GUYANA / VENEZUELA

Title: Back to the Soil

Subtitle: A Journey of Resilience and Hope

Author: CULTURE OF BLESSINGS INC/ Bibi Alli

Editor-in-Chief: Ediclia Bastardo de Persaud / **https://somospersaud.com**

Book design and layout: Ediclia Bastardo

Proofreader: Marie Annand

Cover design: Levi González/ @levisuales/levisuales@gmail.com

ISBN: 9798353091325

Independently published

FOREWORD

Imagine you have nothing to eat; I mean nothing; no half bag of pasta in the cupboard, no bread or vegetables, NOTHING.

There is dry dusty scrubland to cultivate but you have no seeds to plant nor tools to use. No one can help you because they have nothing.

Now you are ready to appreciate the stories this book has to tell.

My involvement began in the Autumn of 2020. I had sent two of my books to Darko Emmanuel in Ghana for the children there to enjoy. In doing so, I learnt of two young boys who were struggling against the odds to revive their little vegetable garden which had been decimated by animals. Their faith and determination overwhelmed so much, that I decided to help in any way I could and thought of one day writing a little book about their challenges.

Fortunately, Mrs. Bibi Ali, head of the Culture of Blessing, had also heard about my boys. She was born into an extremely poor family in very similar circumstances. As an adult she founded 'Culture of Blessing', an incredible organization, which offers help to many in the most vulnerable countries, enabling them to grow crops and vegetables to feed their families.

She proposed that a Culture of Blessing Team should gather stories from a handful of those from different countries who have little on this earth but the will to survive.

Thus, the idea for this book was born.

Prepare to be thrilled by the tenacity of the young boys Bernard and Oscar, heartbroken by the plight of families like Larry's and Evelyn's but then immersed in and overjoyed by their personal triumphs. Meet Paul Oyo who champions the need for better conditions in Uganda offering healthcare to orphans, widows, and the elderly.

Each story will draw you straight into their world to see and experience it for yourself.

The joy I feel every time I video call my boys and their families in Ghana is something I shall always treasure.

There is much to be learned from all those who are featured here. They help us to gain a fresh understanding and insight into the problems faced in the severely impoverished areas of the world.

If nothing else, it helps us to ask ourselves the right questions about how we can help.

Finally, my heartfelt thanks to Bibi Ali and the **Culture of Blessings INC** who work tirelessly to bring hope, help, and encouragement to many families in many parts of the world.

Marie Annand

Table of Contents

DEDICATION

To those children and young people of the world who must work the land to help provide food for the sustenance of their families

To all families who have been left behind because of poverty and situations that make them vulnerable in society.

To the new generations so that they do not lose hope and go back to the soil that gives them provision and life.

To the wonderful Culture of Blessings team who has made it possible for us to share these wonderful stories and experiences.

ACKNOWLEDGMENT

I would like to express deep gratitude to the participants of each story told in this book, especially the children, who with simplicity and unconditional love narrate their resilient experiences.

Thanks to all those directly or indirectly involved in the production of this book, **Darko Emmanuel** from Ghana, and **Paul Oyo** from Uganda, who have been the liaisons between Culture of Blessings INC and the communities mentioned.

Special thanks to **Ediclia Bastardo** from Venezuela, who worked tirelessly on this book's editing, narration, interior design, and publication, not to omit the valuable intervention of **Marie Annand** from the UK, who provided invaluable support in the editing process.

I must ratify that the wonderful team of Culture of Blessings INC whose members joined forces and focused all their energy and commitment on the project despite living in different parts of the world. Thank you very much

I thank the contributors and sponsors of Culture of Blessings INC.

I also want to acknowledge the **UjimaNia Lions Club** in Brooklyn of which I am a member, for the great work done through the years

Another great organization I would also like to mention is the **Arthur Ashe Institute for Urban Health** of which I have been a member for 22 years and with which I have grown as a human being through the wonderful community work done over the years. Happy 28th Anniversary. I am honored to be part of your legacy.

Thanks to my entire family the great Alli Family, especially my children and grandchildren, who are the fuel that ignites my motivation to continue my journey and create a meaningful legacy for future generations.

Last but not least important, a warm thank you to the Khan family and the Springer family who are my extended family and have a special place in my heart.

Bibi Ali and Back to the Soil

I compare the seasons of my life to that of a seed being planted to that of now being a fruit to make a difference in the lives of others, my stages of growth and development. Coming out of a lifestyle of abject poverty, which had shown no indication of any possibility whatsoever of anyone in my family ever seeing a positive outcome in the future. It was my determination and fortitude to survive such an existence that prompted me to plant some vegetable seeds and become a street vendor hawking my vegetables and fish on the streets of Windsor Forest and Ogle in Demerara, Guyana, that would eventually lead me out of the quagmire of an extremely disastrous way of life. Faith and perseverance would eventually guide me to a brighter future in Venezuela; and finally, to a very successful way of life and career in the United States of America

Childhood

I was born in a rural village called Windsor Forest, located on the West Coast of Demerara, Guyana on South America's North Atlantic coast on November 10, 1960. The village, which is part of a cluster of other small villages, is about 40 minutes by bus to Georgetown, the capital of Guyana. It is so small that it could be driven around in one day. Windsor Forest is known as an agricultural farming community where most of the people grow mainly rice, sugarcane, and other cash crops such as fruits and vegetables. Most of the residents own cows and chickens in their backyards. It wasn't anything unusual to see a cow, sheep, or dog running around all over the place. In Windsor Forest, most of the people there relied a great deal on cow's milk which came from their cows, and for those who had sheep, they survived because of those animals – the chickens and the eggs – and all those animals were fed with organic products. The chickens were fed with rice and other food that was thrown at them, and they walked around and pecked around the yards. For some people who had one or two cows, they would give them water with a little rice flour mixed in, which would be like a kind of porridge. They would also take the cows to the back of a dam – an open field where they grazed. Each homeowner that had a cow would have a brand with a number on the back of the animal and so whenever anyone saw that particular brand, they knew they couldn't trouble that cow. Another curious thing about those cows, it seemed as though they were so smart that they knew how to get back home to where they belonged. Most often, milk cows that had calves, those calves would be raised to later provide beef, and this would be done where the animals would be slaughtered every week. Although I was brought up in a Muslim family, the community where I grew up consisted of other religious faiths and ethnic groups. However, what we learned about the religions was primarily through my adopted maternal grandparents. In Windsor Forest, all I could see around me was nothing but hardship and two troubled parents running here and there trying to make a dollar to maintain a family. My father, Abass Alli, was a rice farmer and his family also worked in farming that went way back. He later went to work as a laborer at the Guyana Rice Development Board in Georgetown. We had no permanent place to live; every month we were moving somewhere else. My mother, Bibi Shakoora Baksh, was originally from a place called Mahaica Creek, a big farming community in Demerara. She and my father did not have a stable life and never owned anything. What I could see was that their life was sad, and they were always bitching and arguing with each other. Theirs was not a happy home. They were just a sad couple. They never got along because of my father, who was always drinking. I did not know how what seemed so simple would affect me later on in my life. Our home life was one in which we were always planting, and wherever we went, we were planting. Mama was a woman who always knew how to plant, and we as children always planted for our food. Because of that, Mama was able to survive in raising her children. We were fed a lot of milk and rice; Mama would boil the rice, then add milk and sugar to it – to me, that was cereal. Food would be available in the backyard and front yard, and fish would be caught in what we called the "trench" which we called "sweet water" (or freshwater) fish. Where we lived then was not far from the river which was a couple of blocks away from the Atlantic Ocean

But, for folks living in Demerara, we mostly were able to survive most of the time without having a regular doctor in our community. People didn't go to the doctor, and quite often, whenever someone got very sick, they'd just simply die because of a lack of proper treatment. But, in the Indian culture, we were a lot into the use of natural medicines. If someone had an earache, they would have some leaf that would be squeezed and put into the ear, or they would put some oil in the ear; if someone had a cold, they would use fever grass and other types of bush and boil it and given as a drink. So, there was always something that they would have that was natural-based that was used as a drink that usually worked. In those days when we were growing up, if we saw someone sick, or if a child was sick, usually they didn't have the opportunity to explain to their parents just how they felt, because quite often, the parents themselves would be so confused on their own to know exactly what to do. In my case, if I had a headache, I would usually keep my mouth shut or sometimes maybe I didn't even have time to feel the headache. So, in my mind, it was all about me waking up every day, where we had cows, chickens, and fruits. We ate what our parents had to offer — and usually, we didn't even know how they found the food — or whatever was made and given to us we ate. In such a situation, it was left up to a young girl to figure out what to search for because there was nothing else to do, and I was forced to search for what was around the yard or go on the street. In my head, I didn't think a lot of the children in my neighborhood were anything like me, personally, because they all came out of different homes, and to me, their homes were a little better balanced. And as far as education goes.

I went to school without shoes, and for that matter, most children in my community in those days walked around barefooted. When I finally did manage to get a pair of shoes, I treated them like they were made of diamonds. It wouldn't be until I left Windsor Forest and moved to the other side of town that our life would become a little better and I would then be able to finally get a pair of shoes and not have to walk barefooted. I ended up with a little education from what would be the equivalent of junior high in America. As far as clothing went, I didn't have a lot of dresses; family members would give Mama clothes, but I can only remember having one or two dresses. I didn't have a lot. In those days I had my home dress, and since we had nowhere to go as my parents couldn't afford to take us to any movies or go on outings to too many places where we would have to dress up.

Mama had her little kitchen garden. We had cows and my great-grandmother used to milk the cows. We were able to survive because of the vegetable garden and the few things that we were able to buy such as rice. In those days, people didn't eat a lot, but we ate good but natural foodstuff; in the mornings we would eat some roti or some vegetable from the garden and that was the kind of food that kept us. We would drink milk from the cows and that milk kept us healthy I think that's probably why I didn't see any sickness in the family because the little that we were eating was natural. There were also so many fruits around the yard that we ate and those fruits kept us healthy.

My siblings and I were happy kids in our world and we were happy because I always wanted to be outside selling and I always had my brothers and sisters around me while I was selling. I think it was fun for them to sit around while they saw me selling whatever it was I selling, and I felt like I was a leader to them. They would always listen to me and they all grew up with me, which was part of that fun and excitement for them. Our parents were off in their little world and as such, they didn't pay as much attention to us, especially since our father was an alcoholic and we were afraid of him – there was always that fear. As far back as I can remember, my father was always drinking and never took care of his responsibilities to his family. Whenever Mama asked him for money, he would already have drunk his money after he got paid. I think that's where their problem came from and so it was always a continual struggle for mama. It would be during such times whenever Papa got drunk that I would take my brothers and sisters and run over in the middle of the night to our great-grandmother's house that was just down the street from where we lived because we felt safer there. As a young girl, I always knew how to get away from danger. I always looked after my brothers and sisters from that young age. As I got older, papa drank more and it was getting worse by the day. Whenever he was not drinking, he could appear to be the best father there ever was. He would cook – and he was a good cook – he would cook curry chicken, cook-up rice, or a fish curry; he was entertaining and happy, but it was something we didn't see very often. Those were the few pleasant and memorable times. I don't know what he would be angry about other than maybe it was the alcohol that was in his system that made him behave that way.

As you can see, I grew up amid adversity, poverty, and abuse, and yet hope never left me. I was able to survive amid a constant struggle. As I grew up I understood that there were other options and ways of life and that somehow, I could find them. As I mentioned, we grew our food in the backyard, which taught me how to grow and respect plants. I learned to plant, take care of, and harvest all kinds of vegetables and I took some of them to school and also to the surroundings of my community to sell them, my siblings always accompanied me and were my biggest fans.

The constant search for better life options led me to emigrate, develop myself as a person, obtain a better income, and help the rest of my family.

At the age of 16, I emigrated to Venezuela where I worked and struggled to establish my own business, which turned me into an economically independent woman, but the challenges were just beginning. Later I moved to the United States where I remain, enjoying my children and grandchildren, still trying to build a solid legacy in which love, coexistence, helping and sharing, and above all love and respect for the land that nourishes us predominate.

A few years ago, I wrote and published my first book, called The Power of the Earth, in which I recount, in detail, much of my life's journey. Eventually, I founded Culture of Blessings INC, through which we reach out to communities and individuals in vulnerable situations to restore hope by offering our support both materially and through entrepreneurship workshops. **Back to the Soil** is our second book, "our" because Culture of Blessings is a great work team, formed by men and women from different latitudes, who have believed in my project and now contribute and work to strengthen the objectives and goals of the organization.

I wanted to share part of my story, like that of a little girl, who like the children we refer to in this book, also went through adversities but did not lose faith, and life has shown her that there is Power in the Soil, so let's get to know a little more about those wonderful human beings who are following the legacy and have returned to the soil.

BACK TO THE SOIL
GHANA
My Little Square Meter Garden

My Little Square Meter Garden

I would like to introduce the main characters and the scenario of the stories you are about to read. Let's embark on this wonderful adventure.

The events took place in Asiakwa, Accra, the capital of Ghana in the East of Africa.

GHANA

For those who are uncertain, Ghana is a country in West Africa. It's nestled between Cote d'Ivoire on the west and Togo on the east. The north is bound by Burkina Faso which is home to the largest elephant population in West Africa and the southern extremes look onto the Atlantic Ocean. At 92000 square miles, its area in similar to that of Great Britain.

Ghana is a fascinating place with a rich history and culture. It is Africa's second-largest producer of gold and, not surprisingly, was once named The Gold Coast. It is also the world's second-largest producer of cocoa.

The capital city, Accra stretches majestically along the Gulf of Guinea. It boasts glittering beaches, monumental buildings, museums, galleries, and much more, but sadly, it is a different story in many of the poorer suburbs.

Those coming from rural areas to find work in the cities often end up living on the streets in a state of destitution, with rent and food prices being too high for them to afford.

Many children are forced to walk the streets homeless trying to make a living without the food, shelter, and education they are entitled to.

One such rural area is Asiakwa a small farming community lying about 50 miles northwest of Accra. The work in the area is mainly restricted to mining, farming, and petty trading.

Water is piped from the river and then treated but the water is polluted from the mining activities further up where mercury is often used in the process.

Access to adequate housing and proper sanitation facilities continues to be a problem.

Education is very basic. Books and any extra lessons must be paid for but for the majority, this is out of the question financially.

Thus, although the level of poverty has improved many still live in precarious conditions.

You must know the people who made it possible for this story to reach your hands and of course, the wonderful people who starred in the events that we are going to narrate here.

Introducing Ghana's Stories

B y chance, in the year 2020, parallel events occurred that would mark the lives of persons from different latitudes. Marie mourned the passing of her sister, with whom she had shared many of her dreams and goals, no longer achievable together. Despite the difficulties and challenges faced, Marie managed to publish her book, which was also one of her projects in common with her deceased sister. On the other side of the world, in a small town in Ghana, Africa, Bernard and Oscar were struggling to develop a small garden of barely one square meter, in the courtyard of the house of one of them. They faced challenges and many difficulties. By the grace of God, the lives of those children and Marie's were aligned to coincide, through Darko Enmanuel, who turned out to be the link with **Culture of Blessings INC** and also a true advocate in promoting agriculture and supporting vulnerable sectors.

Darko has been the link between the children and Marie, through him, she has been able to support the children's journey in pursuing their goals.

After the first and second unsuccessful attempts to create the garden, as they called the small portion of land planted, it was possible, with the help of donations, to buy the necessary supplies to cultivate a much larger area in better conditions and with much-needed seeds, materials, and implements.

In January 2021 the building of a greenhouse was begun to prevent the vulnerable seedlings from being destroyed by excessive rainfall.

The results and harvests exceeded expectations, so much, so that other children joined the work and all were able to provide support to their families.

The small garden of one square meter became an extension of more than 400 square meters, which was baptized with the name KIDSFIELD.

In June 2021 Mr. Darko successfully proposed the registration of Kidsfield and the website of the registered foundation was designed. You can check out the website here. https://edarko61.wixsite.com/mysite

KIDSFIELD GH; We're a non-profit organization that seeks to provide humanitarian aid and initiate life-changing projects that will enhance the upcoming generations thus helping them to grow better and transform their lives. In this way, they will be able to reach their greatest heights and use their God-given talents to their highest potential.

We are an organization that is determined to enhance children's experiences, champion their interest in gardening, open up their academic possibilities and improve the quality of life for them and their families.

Bernard's Background

I am Bernard Boateng, born on December 3rd, 2006 in Accra, a rural region in Ghana to my parents Agnes Boatema and Alex Aboagye. My father is a Barber and my mother is a trader who sells groceries in our neighborhood. They had three children, two sons and a daughter, of whom I am the youngest.

We lived in one room in the suburbs of Accra. The high city rents and inflated food prices made life a constant struggle.

We moved due to my parent's health issues and also because the pandemic brought along economic hardships that made it very difficult to make ends meet. We returned to our extended family in Asiakwa as they would provide support for our living. As a result of basic shortages during the lockdown, the cost of food and other groceries rose to levels we could barely afford.

State education here is greatly lacking in teaching and learning materials such as textbooks, storybooks, and basic equipment. There are no libraries or computer access and often the teachers are poorly informed and not supported.

To be enrolled in a private school, which is far better in terms of the quality of education than the public schools, about 600 Ghs must be paid for admission and thereafter around 300 Ghs for an academic term. This comes to about 1200 Ghs for the academic year. For the majority, this is impossible unless a sponsor or guardian is on hand to help.

I will let you know what has happened from the beginning of the pandemic period until now.

Bernard's Garden Journey

My interest in gardening began amid the pandemic, in May 2020; also, around the time, we moved to the city. I always had so much love for plants and have always admired the way crops grow to yield the food we eat.

My interest in gardening began during the pandemic, in May 2020, after we moved from the city. I always have had so much love for plants and have always admired the way crops grow to yield the food we eat.

I woke up early one morning and decided to create a garden designed to be supportive of our kitchen. I worried about having enough space as it was very limited but it did not hinder my dreams from pushing their way up through the earth and reaching proudly towards the sun, much like the crops I wished to grow; all this to have a garden to support my family. I desperately wanted to help them. I loved my life with my grandparents so much. I was greatly troubled by their lack of food with so many mouths to feed.

I told my grandmother who was up early too, as old people often are. Delighted, she gave me some corn seeds and I rushed off to my little patch.

In the process of planting the seeds, Mr. Darko Emmanuel, whom I had recently met came to me and gave me additional seeds. He said they were certified so more standardized than those from my grandma. I was delighted to have them.

Mr. Darko's own words about that time:

"I was staying with Samuel Yeboah's family, Bernard's cousin, who introduced me to Bernard. My first encounter with him was one morning when I walked out of the room and noticed him trying to sow some corn seeds on the hard surface soil. That was when I gave him some certified seeds.

Thereafter, I started providing him with some vegetable seedlings which I had collected from my farm. Not long after, Oscar joined Bernard to champion the dream. The kids showed much passion in what they were doing and they asked me to join the farm permission was granted by their parents for them to go with me. They became a helping hand to me and also helped me to get the irrigation pipes fixed and they sometimes encouraged me to join them on the farm, even when I was feeling down. I genuinely have so much love for them as they were so committed towards the soil".

Oscar Appears on the Scene

As time went on I made extensions to the garden. I had support from my mother. She helped me make fences around it. Then I met Oscar who used to live in Asafo Akyem. but also moved to Asiakwa. He said he preferred living in Asiakwa because he enjoyed so much being with his grandfather. He is now like a brother to me. Oscar joined me on the journey and he was so passionate about gardening as well. Our focus on the little garden became very very strong.

Darko Emmanuel kept providing seedlings for us, such as eggplants and peppers.

Only 65 days after planting we started reaping the fruits of our labor. It made our families so happy and proud of our immense effort. It was delightful to eat from our little garden.

This made our passion and enthusiasm increase. Our garden looked greener than the rest of the gardens in our community.

BERNARD AND OSCAR

MY LITTLE GARDEN

MAY/2020

Disaster on the Field/0ct 2020

One day we woke up and, happily unaware of the disaster about to unfold, we strode down the dusty road leading to our vegetable garden. We noticed that some animals had invaded the garden. They were feeding on the crops! It hurt us and the garden very badly. Our spirits were low. It was such a sad incident.

After finding our optimism once again, we decided to do repairs. There were still a few crops left so we did maintenance on the fence to protect them. Mother, Oscar, and I joined forces to get it fixed as soon as possible. We even had grandmother sew sacks to be used as fencing materials.

However, even after all of our hard work, a few days later some sheep invaded the garden. A second invasion! The sheep destroyed our fencing materials and ate the few plants we had left in the garden.

Frankly, we were worried and sad. We cried that very morning. Oscar and I were upset about it. Mother and grandma were worried about the challenging times we were facing.

Our guide Mr. Darko arrived and noticed the sad incident and the tears on our faces. He gave us hope and motivation, saying we should not give up as we were going to build it up again. It seemed hard, as we had nothing left to build it back, but his words inspired us.

He told us that there will always be challenges in life and being aware of that would help us become stronger than before. It would help us face any challenge thrown at us and it would make us stronger if we never gave up on our goals.

DISASTER ON THE FIELD

A Garden with Friends/Building a Greenhouse

A couple of weeks later, around October time, Mr. Darko gave Oscar and me a nice storybook. It was written by Marie Annand, a Scottish teacher. The tales in the book were so fascinating! Reading is one of my hobbies so it was incredible to have such a nice book shipped to us in Ghana, all the way from Scotland.

We became friends with Miss Marie, forming a strong connection. Mr. Darko told her all about the devastation of our garden and how we were trying to solve the problem. She felt our pain and, out of the generosity of her heart, decided she would sponsor us and help build a brand-new garden.

Thus began the organization. We realized we could make a bigger and better garden than before. We moved to a bigger area, then we invited our friends and neighbors to join us. We made lists of the materials we would need to make progress and they were provided for us very shortly! We had tomatoes, peppers, eggplants, lettuce, carrots, watermelon, cucumber seeds, and more.

We were about eight kids in total, along with Mr. Darko, clearing bushes and preparing the field. Our friends had become fascinated by our little garden when we decided to do the expansion. They began to show interest and help us clear the bush as we started the land preparation for the field.

In this way, with a lot of work, perseverance, and determination, our little garden resurfaced and became the **KIDSFIELD**, as we have called it, which is one of the most beautiful and largest in our community. The most important thing for us is that we have produced enough vegetables to help support our families and even to share with those most in need.

The year 2021 began with great enthusiasm and expectations. We already had the support of our mentor, Marie, who was aware of any shortages and could help out while keenly watching our progress. Mr. Darko was in charge of keeping her abreast of all the details through photos and videos, some of which we share with you in this book.

In January we began to build a beautiful greenhouse to protect the seedlings and germinating seeds from the rain, allowing the sun's rays to properly nourish our plants.

I will never forget the joy and encouragement that the entire team showed at every step of our journey. There was no lack of cooperation and a good attitude, as entrepreneurs and leaders of our kidsfield.

The fruits of our effort did not wait and we obtained a harvest throughout the year.

In June, Mr. Darko and Marie took the necessary steps to register a non-profit foundation, KIDSFIELD/GHANA, with the relevant institutions.

During this process, we have learned what are the necessary steps to produce a bountiful harvest. These include planting in metal cans, preparing compost to nourish the land, and building a nursery to protect our seeds, both from rain and from different pests which cause infection. We know the cycle of transplanting, watering, keeping the plants healthy, and of course harvesting which returns to the preparation of the land for the planting of new crops.

We also shared our knowledge with other children from other neighborhoods, even those who did not have enough space in their homes, using creativity and different strategies to make the most of resources and small spaces

The team grows / Clearing the bush

Building the Greenhouse/
Working hard

Sponsoring Bernard and Oscar

Today we have Marie's support, not only about the Kidsfield and some basic needs of our families but also with education, since she is also kindly sponsoring our schooling.

We felt blessed to have such great momentum, it was like a dream come true!

Marie's words:

"I am so proud to be part of the kidsfield team and feel privileged to have played a part in its development. I have watched my financial support buy the necessary seeds, fences, hoses, equipment, and more to help the children achieve their dream.

Bernard and Oscar are benefiting from the extra schooling and books they now have. I am delighted with their progress. In this too they are hard working.

Their determination to come back when their little garden was decimated by animals impressed me so much as did the encouragement and help of Emmanuel Darko who first made me aware of their plight.

It's been so heartwarming to speak to and see them on video calls. They just burst with energy and enthusiasm. The commitment in the early days and, now that their friends have joined, the commitment of the team is so inspiring.

The videos I see show the difficult conditions they work under, young boys breaking up the hard earth with pickaxes, cutting down the bushes with cutlasses, and nursing the seedlings in tin cans inside the self-made greenhouse.

I am so proud, especially of Bernard who is in charge now, and Oscar who is his right-hand man. Mr. Darko plays a huge part with his help, encouragement, and hard work on the website.

Of course, they reap what they sow and their harvests are amazing. I clap my hands in joy when I see the pictures.

In the future I would like to see all the team sponsored in their education as I do with Bernard and Oscar, more awareness made out with the region of what they are achieving and perhaps them being able to travel to other regions to encourage other children to do the same, championing the cause!!

We need sponsorship or donations here and in other regions to kick start the project there and help the kids grow vegetables to feed their families.

Bernard's team now has hopes of feeding their families and selling some of the fruits of their labors, so that they may become self-sufficient and possibly more!!

I am privileged to be part of their dream, to see it unfold, and to see with much pride what amazing young people they truly are"

SPONSORING / BOOKS
CULTURE OF BLESSINGS

A Journey of Resilience and Hope
Marian Manu Gyimaa

Marian at the age of three was transferred from Princess Marie Louise Children's hospital to the Korlebu Teaching Hospital for treatment of difficulty in breathing and recurrent episodes of fever.

The doctors at Korlebu Teaching Hospital confirmed an obstructive sleep apnea and grade 3 tonsillar hypertrophy and, as a result of her condition, she needed an urgent surgical procedure known as adenotonsillectomy (removal of both the adenoid and the tonsils).

Due to her financial background, Marian was unable to receive the necessary medical treatment. Mrs. Gladys Abena Owusua, a health officer at the hospital, got to know about Marian's case through Mr. Darko Emmanuel who is a friend of hers.

Marian's mother, Sarah Lambon, is a small trader who moved from Atebubu, in the Brong Ahafo region, to Accra to try to make an income. The case came to the attention of Social Welfare through the Health Promotion Manager, Mrs. Ruth Allotey, and Gladys Abena Owusua. Fortunately, Social

Welfare was able to waive around 64% of the total bill for Marian's surgery.

Sadly, although the hospital's Social Work was able to cover a significant part of the total cost, the girl's parents did not have sufficient resources to pay the rest. The situation generated a lot of stress and despair in the mother and the family.

Luckily, through Claire Arnold a friend of Darko Emmanuel, the family got to know Gerry Gallacher, a Scottish Humanitarian, who agreed to help fundraise the remaining amount for the surgery. The surgery was successful on the 27th of January 2021, and Marian is currently strong and free from any throat infection.

Darko Emmanuel has become an important link between the organizations which have financially supported Marian's surgery.

Marie Annand, who has been active in regards to the foundation of the **Kidsfield**, also represents a solid base in sponsorship and support of the children, including Marian, especially after the surgery, as her parents find it very difficult to cover even their basic needs.

Currently, Marian is 5 years old and attending kindergarten 2 in Mount Zion, Taifa-Accra. Although Marian is now well, life has not been easy. Therefore, sustainable help for her and her family is imperative to improve her quality of life in terms of nutrition, education, and health.

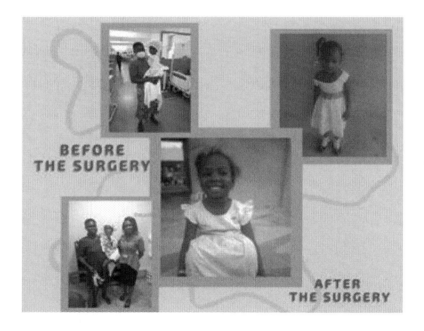

BEFORE THE SURGERY

AFTER THE SURGERY

David Larry Yakubu's Farming Journey

M r. David Larry Yakubu was born in 1958 in Najong Number 2, a small Village in the Northern region of Ghana. His parents were local farmers. He attended basic and elementary school in Najong Number 2 and completed this in the year 1980. He settled down with his wife in the year 1981.

In 1990 Larry attended a child care course in Bolgatanga, in the Upper East Region, which was run by the presbytery Mission. After the course, he was employed as a village health worker with the presbytery Missionary at Makango, 29 km from Salaga in the Northern region of Ghana.

During that era, a conflict rose between the Gonjas and the Komkombas tribes, and the head pastor of the mission was killed. As a result of the conflict, which had caused much tragedy, the work was abandoned. Larry and his family moved from Makango to a village called Fuu in the same northern region.

After his migration, he had very little and so had to restart a new life with his family. Having no job, he acquired some farming land and engaged himself with his family in subsistence farming, growing crops, and rearing animals for family consumption. They also earned a living from the sales of some of the produce. Life was very hard as they were very small scale unlike those who run commercial farms.

Mr. Larry and his family now grow grains such as rice, maize, sorghum, soya bean, cowpeas, and vegetables such as peppers, okra, tomatoes, and other leafy kinds. They also rear animals such as pigs, local fowls, and goats.

He said, "Finding myself back to the soil has helped me and my family to be free from the burden of hunger. Even if we have no money, we can still eat."

The most challenging situation is, as he is quite poor in terms of money, he and his family are often not able to hire a tractor so, they clear the land and till the soil themselves with tools like hoes and cutlasses, so they can farm.

Even in times when they can hire a tractor, outgoings such as the cost of seeds, pesticides, and fertilizers become challenging for them. This sometimes causes them to be late in starting the farming season and they cannot reap the maximum yield as expected.

The little money they earn from the sales of their products must also be used to cater for the children's school bills, the house upkeep, and other needs and necessities so they can't afford to buy all that is necessary to support their farming endeavor.

Mr. Larry said "Mostly we have the energy, the passion, and the desire to farm on a bigger scale, but we have no available support which would empower us to do so.

My wife is one of the strongest women in the world. I call her a workaholic who can work from 9 to 5, 24/7. She's been so supportive and I can't share my story without making mention of her love, passion, and sacrifice for the family. Without her supporting energy, life would have been so much worse.

We have 5 children, two boys, and three girls. We had 8 children but 3 passed away. Our oldest daughter is enrolled in the nursing college from which she could soon qualify as a nurse but her school fees are becoming very challenging for us to meet. The child after her is our eldest son, Abraham. He is a mason and peasant farmer and has been very helpful on the farm. The next daughter after Abraham is a seamstress, and our youngest daughter is in the senior high school at Tamale. Our younger boy is currently in 6th grade, primary school.

I hope and pray to see them all grow up to be great people, learning from us but becoming more successful and attaining new heights. I am so delighted and fascinated to share my story in **'Back to the Soil',** with the help and support from **Culture of Blessings INC**. My family and I are making our journey in life using the power of the soil"

Mr. Larry and his family on their farm

Marie Annand

My name is Marie Louise Annand. I was born in the year 1955 in a town called Inverness which nestles around the mouth of the River Ness in the north of Scotland.

I teach mathematics to secondary school children and write poetry about the myths and legends of Scotland for children and adults.

The seeds of my journey with Kids fields began in lockdown just as those same seeds were being sown into the lives of two little boys, Bernard and Oscar, in Ghana. These seeds would turn our paths around so that they would inevitably cross before the end of that same year.

My sister was diagnosed as terminally ill in January and, a brilliant felter of toy animals, pictures, and scarves, she now found herself unable to continue because of pain and weakness in her shoulders.

One evening together I wrote a poem dedicated to her and her amazing skills. When I read it out, she loved it so much I was ordered to read her more of my stories. She urged me to publish my work and we spent the next day excitedly looking up publishers locally and making plans.

Sadly, not long after in March, she passed away but I was determined to carry on and keep our dream alive.

I found a publisher, a charitable organization in Inverness, who could help despite the lockdown. I found a young enthusiastic illustrator who worked for them and we set about creating my book.

It finally came out in August 2020. It was a book of little stories written in verse for children.

Family and friends rallied around to share its publication on social media.

It just so happened that a member of my family had been to Ghana in 2018 where her friend and guide was Emmanuel Darko who champions families' needs in the area. Mr. Darko was then in touch with Culture of Blessings INC, which has been the link to reach the children.

He commented on the book, and I replied and arranged to send two of them for the children in Ghana.

Soon after I excitedly watched a video of a young lad Bernard reading from one of them in that distant land. I was so proud of us both!

Impressed and overwhelmed by his determination, I kept in touch from that day onwards.

When I learned that his vegetable garden had been destroyed for a second time I gave financial support so they could make a fence around a new and better garden which we called Kidsfields. I helped finance more seeds and tools for the boys then watched as more became interested and the project grew.

Mr. Darko told me about the education in the country and how Bernard would benefit from having his books and extra lessons so I decided to sponsor him. That was in February 2021. Following this, I also sponsored Oscar to help him buy books and receive extra lessons, in August 2021.

Darko Emmanuel

Darko is a farmer, entrepreneur, advocate, volunteer, and humanitarian from Ghana, West Africa. He's the founder and director of Go Agro Farms and Consultancy Limited, a farm brand and consulting company for agribusinesses. Darko Emmanuel has developed so much passion for serving the needing people and communities in Ghana since the year 2016. He's the co-founder and former C.E.O of the National Readers Association, an organization that enhances the sustainability of quality education by promoting literacy in Ghana, through the establishment of libraries in rural communities and the encouragement of reading programs

Darko has worked with other non-profit organizations and volunteers and has made an impact on uncountable lives in over 100 rural communities, schools, and hospitals with his interventions. He has worked with Ceciyaa Foundation, making provisions for others to have basic human needs such as water, clothing, medical care, educational materials for learning, and famine supplies to support the rural livelihood communities.

The emancipation of poverty, hunger, malnutrition, and ensuring quality education has been Darko Emmanuel's mission as a humanitarian whose sole purpose is to create a world that is stable, equitable, and has the diverse interests of all people.

How did the 'KidsField' project start?

After the destruction of the little garden we had before, we intended *to build back better and stronger than before*. Fortunately for us, we were motivated and supported to rebuild from scratch by Marie and Darko. Mrs. Bibi Alli, C.E.O of the Culture of Blessings Inc., has been championing our goals for sustainable living, with the vision of achieving zero hunger as we plant crops to produce food, in this way demonstrating **the power of the soil** to ensure food security.

Moreover, with the Culture of Blessings, we've been able to organize more outreach activities in Ghana, empowering families by giving them support and providing them with food and other basic human needs.

What do they hope for?

They hope for quality education, sustainable living, and support for their **kidsfield** family to pursue their dreams and goals in life by championing their potential and abilities. They would also like to be entrepreneurs by establishing more business opportunities and companies, so the upcoming generation could reach their God-gifted talents, skills, and dreams.

CULTURE OF BLESSINGS TEAM

We now want to share their story, so the world knows how their wonderful dream for **kidsfield** has grown from such a tiny beginning as a mere square meter of earth to the 400 square meters they cultivate today.

As Bernard and Oscar grow taller and their army of helpers grows larger we hope that other children in rural areas can be helped and encouraged to do the same to end the hunger so prevalent in these regions.

The story of these children demonstrates the power of perseverance, determination, and teamwork, without discarding the importance of timely help as a means of motivation and support amid a global humanitarian health crisis. We see how they use the obstacles in their lives to fuel their desire to help their families and positively impact their community.

This is their story and the story of the trials their families face. But also, of the love, joy, and happiness which they breathe through the soul of the community of Asiakwa, Ghana.

BACK TO THE SOIL UGANDA

Hope amid adversity

Introducing Uganda's Stories

The innocence and vulnerability of children touch the innermost fibers of our being, especially if they are children who live in inadequate conditions, deprived, not only of the basic elements of sustenance but also of physical and emotional well-being.

The impact a physical condition has on those who suffer from it affects their quality of life, having repercussions on live projects and plans, and, of course, on all actions that are taken to achieve such projects. Children are equally affected, in such a way that uncertainty and sadness reign in them, since they fail to understand the reason for the misfortune that surrounds them.

It is gratifying to know that not all cases have tragic endings. Sometimes that light appears at the end of the tunnel and restores hope to those who had lost it.

We are pleased to be part of a team that has joined efforts to change the tragic reality of some very vulnerable children of rural areas in Uganda. We need to strengthen the team and resources to be able to go further and reach more communities, adding to the number of people who receive help so they can, in time, once again embrace hope.

Let's learn about the case of several children who were able to smile amid adversity.

Paul Oyo

My name is Paul Oyo, director and founder of St. Mary's Adi Community Health Centre Services, St Mary's Ady Mixed Farm. **It's located in Kibuzi Village, Busaana Sub-County Kayunga District Uganda East**

We offer free and affordable health care services to orphans, widows, and the elderly, especially those living with HIV and AIDS within the Kayunga District. Uganda, East Africa. I am 36 years old, born and raised in Kizubi Village.

I founded the health care services organization 7 years ago because of my humble beginning, being born at the roadside under a tree before my mother could reach the only clinic within 8 km. I was given the second name of "Oyo" which means a child born alongside the road in Luo (my tribe's) culture.

I also belong to St. Mary's mixed model farming and I am a diploma holder in clearing and a forwarding agent.

Kayunga's features

Kayunga District is located in South-Eastern Uganda and has a total land area of 3,443.62 square km and 835.12 square km (23%) of water. 98% are rural areas which makes farming activities favorable

According to the District Planning Unit in 2014, it was reported that children below 18 years constitute 59% of the population, while children below 15 years constitute 53% of the population. Kayunga recorded a total population of 675,566 (321,976 males and 353,590 females).

The people in Kayunga are generally poor, depending on substance farming, and with the privatization of Lake Kyoga, even farming

I grew up practicing farming with my father, mum, and siblings until I joined high school in 1999, ending in 2002, and later on, joined college for my diploma from 2003 to 2005.

Even after getting employed in Kampala the capital city of Uganda, I kept on visiting my family and continued farming. In 2010 I developed a desire to change my impoverished community through agricultural entrepreneurship and eradication of hunger. I came up with a one-acre mixed model farming model in Kibuzi my village. This consists of growing vegetables, fruits, crops, and rearing animals and birds. I began doing this with children and teenagers from my village.

In 2014 I established St. Mary's Adi Mixed Farm just 200 m from our hospital organization. Due to the HIV and AIDS pandemic in our community for the past year, our village has been hard hit, resulting in more orphans with no support. I could offer these souls to work with us on our farm, to get food and financial help.

With every harvest at **St. Mary's Adi Mixed Farm**, we distribute food to all of our members' families, especially those living with HIV and AIDS. They need more nutritious food to boost their immune system to fight diseases as they take ARVS drugs. At the same time, we sell the supplies to generate money which helps buy scholastic materials for the school children and also to get the household items such as washing soap and detergent, sugar, salt, light candles, etc. Working with these young children is an amazing experience due to their dedication and determination to improve and change their lives.

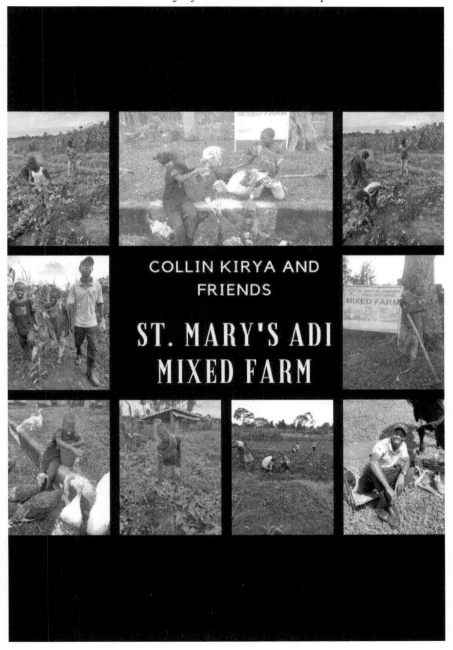

COLLIN KIRYA AND
FRIENDS

ST. MARY'S ADI
MIXED FARM

Collins Kirya

C olin Kirya is 12 years old. He was introduced to me by Beatrice Namulodo, his mother, in 2019, at the age of 9. Collins is the 5th child, out of 9 children. They live with their parents in the same village Kibuzi. Collins is a very hard-working and joyful boy.

Collins Kirya is currently part of our group of entrepreneurs at our farm, St. Mary's Adi Mixed Farm. Collins has also registered vulnerable children whom Mrs. Bibi Alli, founder of Culture of blessings INC sponsors with a variety of seeds for planting. They learn farming lessons at our 1-acre model farming program St. Mary's Adi mixed farm Adi Community Health Centre. This provides a means of getting natural and healthy foods to our patients, providing better nutrition for sick children, especially the very poor, who are amongst the children we teach in the community of kibuzi Village Kayunga District Uganda.

With the help of Culture of blessings INC since 2018 to date, the farm has expanded from just planting foods to a model farming place where the community comes for agricultural entrepreneurship and inspiration training.

Children like Collins Kirya have gained knowledge from the farming method at an early age, which is vital for a child like him so that he be skilled in the future in his sustainability and self-employment.

The farm has also expanded into animal and poultry farming. We can raise chickens, turkeys, ducks, guinea fowls, pigeons, goats, cows, sheep, and pigs thanks to the support funded by Culture of Blessings INC

Concerning our farm, child caretakers, especially Collins Kirya, have been able to reduce costs for the operations, all work being done by them, especially when they are not at school.

We have been able to provide support for the most vulnerable in our community, such as Collins.

It's important to highlight the important role of Culture of Blessings INC in nutrition and provision of clothing, school supplies, and economic support to the Collins family, from the time of the surgery until today.

Farming activities have helped Collins and others like him to learn not only to farm but also to socialize with others children.

Life and work on a farm can be beneficial for adults and children when such work is done safely.

In general, agricultural work for adults is believed to provide exercise, fresh air, opportunities to solve problems, appreciation for the land and animals, and job satisfaction. In farming communities, families are close-knit and support each other in times of need.

Work and learning to take responsibility are good for children and adolescents in all areas of society. Agriculture, in particular, offers many opportunities for young people to develop job skills and benefit from agricultural life.

There are many benefits of growing and working on farms, such as:

> Instills passion, love, and respect for the land.
>
> It forms the character of the person.
>
> Instill a good work ethic.
>
> Teach to take responsibility.
>
> Strengthen family ties and maintain a common project.
>
> Provides ample space for youngsters to play.
>
> Form lasting friendships with other youth.

Simon Wakabi's Background and Health Issues

Young Simon Wakabi is 9 years old, born, and living with HIV and AIDS.

In Kibuzi Village, Busaana sub-county Kayunga District, Uganda, Simon was born and raised in a family of 6, being the youngest. As Simon grew up he started developing sickness which had him admitted to our community hospital. Eventually, our doctors took HIV samples from Simon and his mother which later turned positive.

It was another major blow for her as a single mother of 45, but our council members did their best to advise her and both were later placed on ARVS. With more than 1,000 people currently receiving free health care, food, and household items, thanks to the organization supporting such cases, we were able to support his family.

When Simon reached school age, he was accepted into a local community school. He had the support of our organization and other well-wishers, but he still needs constant help.

Simon has been taking his medication every day before going to school and he has to do so for the rest of his life until HIV gets a cure. It's a bit traumatic but since he's still young he quickly forgets about it. However, he still asks his mum why he has to take medicine every day, morning and evening, before going to sleep, and as a mother, she wants to comfort him by telling him different stories.

At the age of 6 years while at school, Simon experienced a strange vision in his right eye and he could not see at a distance. This later shifted to the left eye. This went on for a year until he became completely blind and dropped out of school. All his dreams of becoming a doctor were shattered. Simon became sad, and he could not understand why all this was happening only to him.

Meeting Simon

One day as he was moving around the community, I passed by the smallest feeder road leading me to one of our St Mary's Adi mixed farms. . I met him and asked him why was he not in school. He then told me, 'Uncle Paul, I can hear you but can't see you. I thought he was joking, as I saw his eyes were widely open, but soon I realized he was right. I led him to their home where I met his mother who explained to me what exactly had happened to his eyes.

I then instructed the doctors of the organization and the community awareness mobilizer, also called Simon, to follow up on the matter and do all the necessary procedures for him to get surgery. They did and I am very grateful to them for their excellent job.

After the required tests were performed in 2019, Simon was referred to Mengo hospital in Kampala, the capital city, specifically to the Eye Department. Along with our friends, we started fundraising campaigns to be able to get him the eye surgery screening, as it's quite costly. At that time, we were looking for a certain amount and we were able to get almost the amount that was needed through one individual sponsor, Dr. Mohammed Arsiwala from Michigan, who was introduced to me by a friend, Mrs. Kathrin Gnilka from Dubai.

Later, Simon was able to have his eye surgery, which was successful and allowed him to be able to see again. Thank God for his sponsor (Mohammed Arsiwala). Then, he rejoined school as he kept going through many tests to find out what exactly caused his blindness. Unconfirmed findings are that it might have been the ARVS he was taking, starting at the very early age of one.

According to the doctors, they have received such cases from many of the patients on ARVS treatments and are still investigating them. Something similar happened in our hospital. We had the same cases of people who were HIV positive and developed cataracts, eventually going blind.

SIMON
WAKABI

SURGERY AND
RECOVERY

BACK TO THE SOIL
VENEZUELA

A purpose in the face of adversity

Purpose in the Face of Adversity

My name is Evelin, I am a Venezuelan and I am about to share just a bit of my story with you.

It was a hot day and apparently, the sunshine was not so appreciated for me. I had dawned in a bad mood due to the continuous worry because of the lack of food, which increased my anxiety, which was silently destroying me. As the person responsible for the household I do not like to share my burdens with the other members of the family, knowing that everyone has their burdens, much less my children. I kept silent, only multiple thoughts went around in my head, looking for a possible solution to such a serious problem.

Thus, my days went by without any apparent solution, only my thoughts accompanied me. Occasionally I would sell some electrical appliances or household goods, which resulted in a momentary solution. Little by little I realized that the house was becoming empty, which increased my anguish. My uncertainty and sadness increased when I thought that I had 26 years working in a public office, in the Government of the State where I was born and currently reside, but the working conditions and benefits had declined steeply. I was falling into depression, which is a disease that appears to be harmless but the truth is that it is predatory, it destroys your motivation, your desire, and your will. It is not easy to cure clinically speaking, only by yourself, with your own strength. This disease makes you lose hope and you begin to deny that something bad is happening. Trying to hide your situation, you live an internal struggle that only you know. In my case, I could not find a viable way out of my situation. One day, talking to my youngest daughter Isabella, she said to me - mom, why don't we plant? - I kept thinking and then I answered her - daughter, do you think so? that is difficult, it implies deforestation and clearing the land, I see it very difficult -. She insisted. - Mom, let's try, it is possible; remember that I did a small planting course - Due to her insistence, I decided to go for a walk to the surroundings of the urbanism where I live and after walking for long minutes inspecting the plots of land, I realized that most of them were occupied by plantings of my neighbors and of plot holders who live in neighboring areas. The only unoccupied land did not look good for planting as it was full of huge stones and buried metal objects. Nothing favored our undertaking as we had no tools either. The only thing we had was my daughter's 'desire' and for fear that she would realize how I felt, I pretended to be optimistic.

That is how the mission began. My daughter was full of encouragement and enthusiasm, which gave me strength. Although inside me, it seemed a difficult task, the commitment to my daughter did not allow me to give up this new project. Despite not having any tools, we improvised some homemade ones. Each step of the process was difficult because there was a lot of brush and more stones than soil, big dry trees, and huge trunks, the soil did not seem fertile. Neighbors and passers-by told us that there was little chance of good fruits, but, even so, we kept on fighting. My daughter's desire was enormous... she thought big, even about exporting fruits to other countries, she saw something big and beautiful. Her daily enthusiasm infected me a little and I realized that the occupation in the preparation of the land made new positive thoughts germinate. A little hope came into our lives, something new to occupy us kept us in a calm attitude, praying at every opportunity that God would open doors of blessing and everything would begin to flow.

Little by little, we felled the trees, cut and cleared the bush, and one by one we removed the large stones, which turned out to be quite heavy. Our hands became calloused to the point that they swelled, we got sunburned, the physical exhaustion became more and more pronounced, and so on for many days.

Every morning, when we woke up and after getting ready, we were carrying not only the implements. I began to notice a slight change in me, a hope was born, and something different and good was flowing. I realized that I no longer spent the day lying down, thinking, and discouraged as I did some time ago, my thoughts were focused on our planting project. I had a new north that directed me to meet the goal of each day since I had committed to finishing the first phase, which was the clearing and deforestation of the land. Sometimes we would work into the night, in shifts While the younger ones did the hard work, I would return home to prepare food for everyone. It seemed that we were close to achieving what I had longed for the most, to finish the clearing and start planting. In our plot, there was an abandoned tank. We cleaned it and made it suitable for bathing since it was as big as a small pool. After each cleaning day, my daughter would go in to bathe, she liked it very much. She told me that this way she recovered new energy and, on several occasions, I accompanied her and I liked to share with her and my nieces there, the water refreshing us and revitalizing us to recover the strength drained by the hard work. On several occasions we were visited by relatives from outside and they liked this place very much. It was something different and, even though we had no experience in planting, we made a big difference among the other plots. We continued in this way until we achieved our first objective, deforestation, and cleaning of our small plot. Without any planting we felt great satisfaction to see our effort crystallized, I never tired of observing it with pride. Many neighbors were surprised, many saw us as incapable of achieving our goal because we are women. They murmured and said that there were 'many issues that we would forget and the matter would come to pass9 that we were not going to plant anything, -those are women from the city, not from the countryside-. The second step that seemed easy turned out to be more difficult and was also done; getting seeds to plant. We went to the farmers' homes in the surrounding area to ask them for guidance on the most suitable crops for the type of land to be cultivated and to try to get them to donate samples of some seeds. The farmers were suspicious and not very receptive. Our attempt in the search was unsuccessful, but we did not give up, we continued our search. When the sun lowered its intensity, we returned in search of seeds to begin planting them, the objective had not yet been achieved, it was more difficult than clearing the land.

Meditating at the dining table, I remembered a biblical text that spoke about the sustenance that our heavenly father provides us and prayed out loud: -Lord you who gives bread to the eater and seed to the sower, then be the one to grant me the seed, because with my strength I cannot-, I waited on Him and immediately His answer was manifested, the glory of God materialized in the provision of seeds. A refreshing sense of relief to feel the hand of the Father. He used a person I hardly knew. On the way home, he commented to me that he was in a crisis as his daughter was going through a very difficult situation and he had no way to help her with food. I told him that my house was quite far away but if he would accept a little help, I could share some food with his daughter and grandchildren. I told him that I did not have much but I could give him half of what I had at home.

We continued talking and it was then that I told him that I had started a project but had not been able to get the seeds for planting. Mr. Andres decided to accompany me to the house so he could take the food to his daughter. We arrived at my house and I shared with him some of the food that was in my cupboard, he smiled and thanked me almost with tears in his eyes. The next day Mr. Andres, out of gratitude, brought me a variety of seeds, such as peanuts, plantain, various types of bananas, tobacco, eggplant, and papaya, among others. He also brought me fertilizer and helped me prepare and nourish the soil. I was very grateful to him for sharing with me important information on how to prepare the land for planting. God's love was manifested there, the answer to my request, a great blessing for me and my family. We continued our planting project with more enthusiasm and hope. We were filled with optimism, I was experiencing a change to continue this beautiful work and, despite all the difficulties, we felt something special when planting trees. We were also planting love for the soil and I was starting a new stage in my life, a new venture. In addition to the need for food, I had an immense need to restart my life, I felt that I had no north because for years I had been immersed in a great depression after suffering several losses of close relatives, including my youngest son, who died by accident and although several years have passed since his death, he was constantly present, his memory reviving a wound that has been difficult to heal. A prayer of faith and clinging to this new beginning gave meaning and hope to many things that had remained unfinished in my life, questions without answers. In this wonderful place, I saw the fruit of my work, of my effort. It is something inexplicable. I have always worked in public administration and when I could not afford the basic household expenses with my salary, an internal struggle grew in me and I thought if the worker is worthy of his salary, why can't I lead a dignified life? That was a big question and here I found the answer, remembering a biblical passage that talks about when Jesus was taxed and He told Peter -go and fish, there you will find a coin in the fish and then pay-, I understood the importance of sowing, there is the sure food, in the sowing, in that power that God gave to the soil to give us that gift, the food, this project was the instrument that God used to free me after living drowned in fear. Once I consolidated my plot of land, I planted several species. Now I have several vegetables planted, but it is not yet time to harvest. We continue to work hard with enthusiasm, although there is no lack of obstacles. The water to irrigate the plants is far away, which makes our work more difficult since we have to carry it in plastic containers.

First thing in the morning, before the sun gets stronger, we leave the house, prepare coffee, take our tools and go to the combat, in search of our blessing, and so six long months passed. One night while we were watching the local news, the president of the Republic made important announcements, not very encouraging for everyone, the covid 19 virus entered the country after several cases were detected, and they declared a worldwide pandemic. Preventive measures began, and a national quarantine was decreed. It was as if the country had gone dark, a very difficult stage began for everyone and especially for us because we had to buy food in the city since we lived in a rural area and to get the transfer to the city wasn't easy. We had to walk two and a half kilometers to take the transport and be able to make any kind of purchase, be it food or other items needed at home.

The time of pandemic brought even more difficulties. Early one Saturday morning I received a call from a sister-in-law asking me to take care of her two little daughters, my nieces,

Jorgelis, 9 years old, and Evelyn, the youngest who bears my name. I had to take care of them for a couple of days, so I accepted, emphasizing that it could only be a couple of days because I did not have enough resources to support the children. After more than a couple of days I decided to call my sister-in-law to come and pick up the girls since it was getting difficult for me to support them. When I managed to communicate with her, I told her to please come and pick up the girls and she answered that she was in 'San Antonio', on the border with Colombia and that the next day she would cross the border... she asked me to please take care of her daughters because she could no longer stand the situation in Venezuela and she could not support them. All this left me speechless, I immediately thought about how I was going to support the girls if I could barely make ends meet. I took a deep breath, I felt overwhelmed again, then I said to my daughter -you who know more about planting, do you think there will be a harvest ready - she took her implements and went to the plot, while I stayed at home quite anxious and worried about not having enough food and now with two more little people at home. My daughter came back about an hour later and told me -mom there is still nothing- I did not expect that answer when suddenly she told me -mom, look behind the door- When I looked out, my biggest surprise was to see that there was a sack with about 30 kilos of cassava. My daughter and I were overflowing with joy, it was a great blessing, I could not get over my astonishment, I could not believe it. It was wonderful to see the fruit of our efforts. Yucca or cassava can be used as a side dish for a variety of meals, it is highly nutritious. That day we prepared it in great quantity, what happiness and tranquility at the same time, a pleasant sensation to see the fruit of our effort, it has no comparison with the adversity that we had to face. It was a joy turned into optimism, into hope, to eat something that we planted with our hands and that for long months we took care of with love and patience. More than food, learning also came, we understood that there was something else to do. Along with adversity comes hope; one must know how to recognize it and make the most of it. These were gratifying moments, because not only my house was benefited, but I was also able to help some relatives and friends. Those results motivated us to continue sowing and looking for more variety of seeds. Now we have 2 more members for the daily work, my nieces, who, with innocence, tenderness, and witty remarks, give a special touch to each day. They have become accustomed to planting and also contribute with valuable ideas. Although they are small, their contributions are appreciated, and they do everything with commitment and love.

We organize ourselves to plant beans, pumpkins, plantains, and bananas, among others. Everything is going well, despite not having the experience we are doing a good job, with difficulties, since, because of the lack of tools, our effort is greater.

One afternoon, after spending days in the city doing personal errands and making some visits to relatives, after eating, and having a little rest, I went to my plot to water, as usual, and I realized that some neighbors had burned something in their yards and as it was summer all the bush was dry. The fire spread to my plot and burned much of the white-water pipes that supplied irrigation, which filled me with anger and a feeling of helplessness to see my damaged pipe after so much sacrifice to develop the distribution of water. It was not easy to see all my work destroyed by the irresponsibility of some neighbors who did not take the necessary precautions and did not even apologize. How terrible it feels to have one's property violated. I felt like complaining, so I sat on the edge of a tree and my discomfort calmed down. I told the girls, let's plant more seeds. That day we planted different types of seeds and cleared bushes, raked and prayed aloud in the field, giving thanks for everything. I felt better, we returned home, I checked my phone and I had a message from Mrs. BIBI ALI. She told me to send my number, she wanted to talk to me. After several failed attempts, I finally managed to communicate with her, it was a pleasant surprise and a blessing for me to know that someone I do not know personally, only through social networks was interested in talking to me. I always liked and read her publications about sowing and her Foundation **Culture of Blessings.** To know that she was interested in me was a great blessing from the Father of lights because all good things come from Him. I felt that it was something beautiful, that I needed it at that moment. I talked to her, and she was kind to me, her soft voice and at the same time strong with hopeful words made me feel how important I am to God, and that He can bless me by any means. She sent me a contribution, so I could purchase some more seeds. I also started a small business that is helping me to multiply the investment and also brings me personal satisfaction. It motivates me to go out and buy the products, show them to the customers and meet more people and I always take the opportunity to talk about what God is doing through the Culture of Blessings. I was also able to repair the water pipe that got burned and I consolidated my planting. Now we have much more, thanks to this valuable contribution. It was not only the money, it was also the encouragement and motivation that brings us personal satisfaction. A new beginning is always important, not only for me but also for my friends and family, since part of my harvest is donated to whoever needs it, whether I know them or not I am always open to helping and sharing with the needy. It is a great blessing the beautiful and meaningful work done by the institution led by Mrs. Bibi. Since then I keep in touch with Mrs. Bibi, for whom I feel great admiration and affection. I follow her work closely and her love for sowing, and I have realized that she is dedicated to helping the needy, not only in Venezuela but in other parts of the world. This has captivated me and transmitted to me that love for the soil, which has the power to give us food. God demands us in his word, not only to share bread but also to provide tools so that other people are motivated to cultivate, and thus together we would eradicate hunger and there would no longer be so much need for bread.

My house has been the home of those in need, despite not being a luxurious house, it is the roof for those who do not have it, and with joy, the door of my house is always open for the needy. There I have sheltered close relatives, my nieces that I am now raising, and now my mother's widower. God rewarded me with two houses. When I had no homes, I asked the Father to help me and I told him that, if he granted me my heart's desire, it would not only be mine but also for those who needed it, and he granted my heart's desire, he provided me with two homes. When we are in gestation we are filled with patience, waiting for the desired fruit for nine long months until the day of birth finally arrives. The same thing happens to us when we plant, we must be filled with patience and wait for such a longed-for moment.

Today, I am writing this story and, just as I am narrating it, God has honored me. Even though I sometimes thought about sharing my story, I saw it as a difficult task, but thanks to Culture of Blessings INC that encouraged me and offered me support, I cannot waste this opportunity. My story will be captured in a book that will be read by several generations, and they can be enriched with such meaningful content. Perhaps for some people, it will be just another story, but for those who open their hearts, it will be a story that will help them understand the importance of perseverance, and that, despite the ups and downs, when God's purpose is to bless you, He uses any means to do so. Nothing is impossible for Him. Even through adversity, I have not doubted God's purpose in my life. I thank God for giving me the wisdom and strength to face every trial and for placing people like Mrs. Bibi Ali and her work team in my life, among whom is my sister Ediclia. She is also part of this wonderful journey, having the task of inserting this story in this wonderful book, **Back to the Soil.**

Venezuela

CULTURE OF BLESSING INC, led by Mrs. Bibi Ali, who was born in a Caribbean country called Guyana, but now resides in the USA.

Mrs. Bibi, through the organization that she leads, has extended her arms of help, in favor of the most vulnerable in some countries, such as Venezuela, Ghana, Uganda, Panama, and her native country of Guyana.

One of the most outstanding achievements of Mrs. Bibi has been the publication of the book **The Power of the Soil,** which is an autobiography, where she expresses and demonstrates that the Soil has the power to revive, feed, and give hope to continue the journey. The power of the Soil is precisely the central theme of the story that concerns us, starring brave, intelligent, and beautiful children from Ghana, specifically in a rural region of Accra, the capital of this country. Remote rural regions of Uganda are also witnessing how uncertainty and despair can turn into hope.

Through CULTURE OF BLESSING INC, a very significant link was established with the countries mentioned and this is how the people involved in this beautiful project, to which I have the honor of belonging, appear on the scene. BACK TO

THE SOIL shares beautiful stories full of courage, faith, companionship, resilience, and above all love. Stories are told by its protagonists and by members of the wonderful team of Culture of Blessings and their collaborators.

Ediclia Bastardo

CULTURE OF BLESSINGS JOURNEY

S ince its founding in 2016 in Valencia, Venezuela, the Culture of Blessings Foundation (Fundación Cultura de Bendiciones, in Spanish) has extended its helping hand to many communities in need, not only in Venezuela but around the world. A few months after its founding, Cultura de Bendiciones became **Culture of Blessings INC** based in the United States of America, and from there continues its altruistic work to other continents.

Recently, Culture of Blessings established an alliance with a foundation based in Uganda, which fights against food shortages and works for the improvement of health services.

Below is a brief overview of this partnership and how to contact them to contribute to this worthy cause.

PROPOSED PARTNERSHIP BETWEEN CULTURE OF BLESSINGS/USA AND GERTRUDE MEMORIAL COMMUNITY HEALTH CENTRE/UGANDA.

Culture of Blessing INC. USA, and Gertrude Memorial Community Health Centre, Uganda will work together, following the visionary reports of development agencies, the World Food Program, and above all the **"UN – Ending poverty and hunger by 2030" an agenda of the Global Food Security and part of the United Nations Sustainable Development Goals – UNSDGs program**. The report calls on all key partners and alliances to come together to shape the evolution of the global food system to end poverty and hunger by 2030.

The report forges a strong connection between agriculture and nutrition which is vitally needed.

Undernutrition remains a daunting challenge worldwide and a stubborn barrier to ending poverty. It is the underlying cause of 45% of under – 5 child deaths

each year and about one in three (1 in 3) children in developing countries like Uganda are stunted. Stunting is an especially pernicious problem leading to long-term harmful effects on physical and intellectual development as well as lower income earning potential over a lifetime, which comprises future human capital and holds back productivity and economic growth.

How do we intend to achieve this?

Gertrude Memorial Community Health Centre will be going into communities and teaching all households how to do small, smart farming in their backyards, specifically targeting nutritious foods and a few birds, for example, leafy greens, broccoli, cauliflower, carrots, eggplants, spinach, and at least 5 hens for a few eggs for the infants' nutrition.

This will be done with determination across all communities and we will equip them with skills and seeds or even give them startup birds at a later stage of this program.

Culture of Blessings and other interested partners will fund this program every month until we create a long-term, sustainable plan.

Project Location on the grid: Nyarurambi Village, Karist Rutoma Nyabbani Road, 150 meters off Kamwenge Mbarara highway, exactly 316.1 km from the capital Kampala, Kitagwenda District.

Contacts:

Whatsapp: +256(0)784955752

On Facebook: James Musinguzi. Gertrude Memorial Community Health Centre.

Email: gertrudememorial@gmail.com

Contact Person: James Musinguzi. Founder and team leader of the project.

Testimonials and Galleries

My name is Michelle Pierre and I am a peasant farmer. I want to share how I met a wonderful woman called Bibi. I met Bibi Alli in July 2017 at a conference in Guyana. After a conversation between us, we realized that we had the same interest in farming and that linked us to a deeper conversation. I shared with her the struggles I was going through to maintain my sowing. She decided to give me a contribution to my farm. I attended a workshop on behalf of Bibi Alli which lasted for two weeks and was based on agriculture. There were thirty-five other participants of various ethnicity and backgrounds. Agriculture has played a big role in my life. My sons are also involved in agriculture. I always believe that when someone grows their own food, they know exactly what they are consuming (from farm to table). Ms. Bibi is a blessing in my life and family. I thank her for all that she has been doing not only for me but for many more people who have gone through hardship.

Michelle in her farm

School in Valencia, Venezuela. 2019

Evelin working on her farm. Her nieces enjoy helping

Wednesday 8th of March, 2022 on **International women's day**
Giving back to the women who have empowered their fellow women in the community.
St. Mary's Adi Community Health Centre Services.org sponsored by the Culture of Blessings INC.

GHANA

Never Stop Dreaming

SOW AND HARVEST

Culture of Blessings and
The Power of the Soil

BIBI ALLI AND FAMILY
A legacy of love for the new generations

SPONSORS

The following people must be acknowledged in this book, as they made a kind and valuable contribution to furthering the work Culture of Blessings has been developing.

Lion Ray Romain

Chioma Lwuagwu

Dr. Simone Lord

Leela Ramasir

Dr. Linda Johnson

Rev. Motie Singh

Margaret Etkins

Dimple Williams

Rev. Joe Persaud

Daly Family

Women Prayer Group "Elohim"

Ladyra Lewis

Rev. Sophie Joseph

Tangerine Clarke

Colette Boston

Jean G. Joseph

"May every sunrise bring you hope and may every sunset bring you joy and happiness"

Lion Rey Romain

How to Contact Bibi Alli and the Culture of Blessings Team

Social Media:

 Culture-of-blessings-Inc

+1 347-822-6960

 culturadebendiciones.org

@culturadebendiciones

A Journey of Resilience and Hope

Made in the USA
Middletown, DE
14 October 2022